T0197500

GOD SAYS: "I am with you Always"

A Children's Book of Comfort

JAN GILL DWYER

Designed by Susan Bolinger

WestBow Press books may be ordered through booksellers or by contacting:

WestBow Press
A Division of Thomas Nelson & Zondervan
1663 Liberty Drive
Bloomington, IN 47403
www.westbowpress.com
844-714-3454

Because of the dynamic nature of the Internet, any web addresses or links contained in this book may have changed since publication and may no longer be valid. The views expressed in this work are solely those of the author and do not necessarily reflect the views of the publisher, and the publisher hereby disclaims any responsibility for them.

Any people depicted in stock imagery provided by Getty Images are models, and such images are being used for illustrative purposes only.
Certain stock imagery © Getty Images.

Designed by Susan Bolinger

Roger Dwyer's photo by:

Roger Dwyer
Country Man Images LLC
Certified Professional Photographer

Scripture quotations taken from The Holy Bible, New International Version® NIV® Copyright © 1973 1978 1984 2011 by Biblica, Inc. TM. Used by permission. All rights reserved worldwide.

ISBN: 978-1-6642-3485-7 (sc)
ISBN: 978-1-6642-3486-4 (e)

Library of Congress Control Number: 2021909940

Print information available on the last page.

WestBow Press rev. date: 08/13/2021

WESTBOW
P R E S S®
A DIVISION OF THOMAS NELSON
& ZONDERVAN

GOD SAYS:
"I am with You Always."

A Children's Book of Comfort

BY JAN GILL DWYER

Designed by Susan Bolinger

Matthew 28:20, NIV
... And surely I am with you always,
to the very end of the age.

When: You walk on freshly mowed grass and notice the teeny tiny flowers and you gaze at them, and you feel ***amazed***.

When: You look at your favorite pet and you see their eyes on you, and you feel *loved*.

When: You hear a grandparent is sick and you can't visit them, and you feel *sad*.

"I am with you always"
When: You go to your piggy bank and it is totally empty, and you feel ***disappointed***.

When: God sends His angels to guard you in all your ways, and you feel *safe*.

When: You see beautiful morning glories in the corn fields and you know God put them there for you to enjoy, and you feel *thankful*.

"I am with you always"
When: Someone you love goes to heaven and you
know you are going to miss them, and you
feel **lonely**.

When: You learn God made all the fruits and vegetables with healthy vitamins and minerals for you to eat, and you feel ***grateful***.

When: Your doggie friend jumps up to say "Good morning, let's play ball!", and you feel ***happy***.

"I am with you always"
When: You are having trouble breathing from a
        cold or virus, and you feel *sick*.

When: You know GOD is just a prayer away, and you feel **connected**.

When: You feel like singing "Yeah! Yeah! Yeah!"
and you realize the Joy of the Lord is your
strength, and you feel ***strong***.

God says; "I AM WITH YOU ALWAYS"
in all these ways and more.

How do you know God is with you today?

Just listen and look for His miracles, and you will realize, YOU NEVER WALK ALONE.

Question: What is a miracle?

Miracles are surprising events or things that take place due to the powers of God. We are surrounded by His miracles. Take a look around you. Listen to God.

In the way the birds sing, the way the squirrels gather nuts for the winter, and the way you see a rainbow after a thunderstorm. You will start to hear and see miracles all around you. Just take time to look and listen for them. You will begin an amazing journey.

Matthew 28:20, NIV
... And surely I am with you always, to the very end of the age.

Psalm 91:11, NIV
For he will command his angels concerning you to guard you in all your ways.

Nehemiah 8:10, NIV

Do not grieve, for the joy of the Lord is your strength.

Mark 10:14, NIV

... Let the little children come to me, and do not hinder them, for the kingdom of God belongs to such as these.

About The Author

Jan Gill Dwyer

Jan has a duel certification, B.S. plus 28 graduate education credits, from West Chester University, in Pa. She furthered her education with the University of the South/ School of Theology/Education for Ministry, under the Episcopal Diocese of Pa. as well as studies in Creative Writing. During the course of her career, she taught Preschool thru 12th grades as well as primary and intermediate Special Needs students. Jan owned and operated an equine therapy program involving mainstreamed summer camps for handicapped and able-bodied children.

She has long been an advocate for children, striving to educate each one to his or her highest potential. She knows God loves all children, red, yellow, black, brown and white, all being precious in His sight. She raised two children, John and homeschooled Joelle, who now together, own and operate a software engineering company, "Matlock & Assoc. LLC."

Jan is presently enjoying being a floating teacher at St Gabriel's Episcopal Church "The Good Shepherd Learning Center," in Douglasville, Pa., writing, and spending as much time as possible with her beloved grandchildren, RaeLynn Sky and Lincoln Jarold.

Also published by the author: "<u>Colors of a City, Philadelphia</u>" available through Amazon.

Designer, Susan Bolinger Susan has a degree in Graphic Design and graduated with top honors from the Art Institute of Philadelphia, Pa. She enjoys freelancing in the graphic arts field. Her other love is horses. Susan dedicates her work for this book in memory of her horse Boone, who took Jan and her on many fine adventures.

Proverbs 16:3, NIV
Commit to the Lord whatever you do, and your plans will succeed.

Printed in the United States
by Baker & Taylor Publisher Services